I0447224

This scorched and tattered flag, recovered from the debris of Ground Zero, hangs in the Office of the Director of CIA. It is a constant reminder of the strength and durability of the nation we serve.

DEVOTION
TO DUTY
RESPONDING TO
THE TERRORIST
ATTACKS OF
SEPTEMBER 11TH

This is the story of how the men and women of CIA responded to the attacks of September 11th. To the extent it can be told in an unclassified account, it offers a sense of the teamwork, creativity, and commitment displayed by Agency officers in the days and weeks after the tragedy. Love of country and dedication to mission sustained them in their vital work.

Most CIA officers belong to one of four Directorates. Each mobilized its unique skills and resources in the wake of the assault on the United States:

★ The Directorate of Intelligence (DI) analyzes information from both open and classified sources to produce timely, accurate, and relevant intelligence. DI analysts help the President and other policymakers reach informed decisions by offering insights on virtually every foreign challenge facing our nation.

★ The Directorate of Science and Technology (DS&T) applies innovative technical solutions to the most critical intelligence problems. DS&T officers design equipment and provide expertise in support of espionage, covert action, and counterintelligence operations.

★ The National Clandestine Service (NCS) is responsible for collecting human intelligence, conducting covert action, and working with foreign liaison services. The Counterterrorism Center (CTC), an NCS component, in cooperation with other US Government agencies and with foreign partners, acts to target terrorist leaders and cells, disrupt their plots, sever their financial and logistical links, and deny them safe haven. Operations officers and analysts serve side-by-side to fulfill CTC's mission.

★ The Directorate of Support (DS) builds and operates facilities all over the world, ensures secure and reliable communications, and runs supply chains that acquire and ship a wide range of critical, clandestine equipment to the most remote corners of the globe.

SEPTEMBER 11 2001
WORLD TRADE CENTER
PENTAGON
SHANKSVILLE

01

On a clear, late summer day, terrorists attacked America. Two hijacked planes flew into the World Trade Center; one struck the Pentagon, and another—headed towards Washington, DC—crashed into a field near Shanksville, Pennsylvania. The attacks claimed thousands of lives and brought home to all Americans a stark reality: our nation faced a deadly enemy, one not only determined to strike but one who saw no distinction between soldier and civilian, man, woman, or child. CIA joined the country in mourning, even as it tracked down those behind the attack.

A group of officers from the National Clandestine Service were in a training course on September 11th; the class was suspended as they started watching coverage of the Twin Towers on a large projector screen. A senior officer stood up and said what everyone felt: CIA would not rest until it brought the fight to those responsible. As he spoke, the scene behind him was the second tower crashing down.

"Nothing will ever be the same."

– CIA Deputy Director John McLaughlin

Previous page: World Trade Center, New York City, September 11, 2001.
Top right: The Pentagon after attack.
Lower right: Shanksville, PA crash site of flight 93.

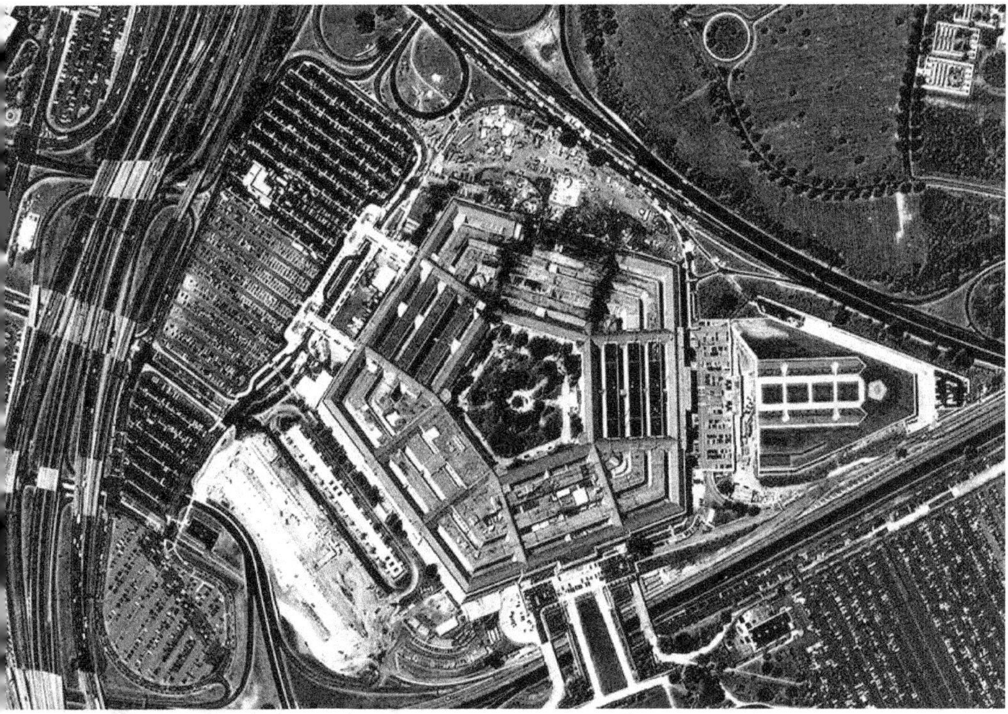

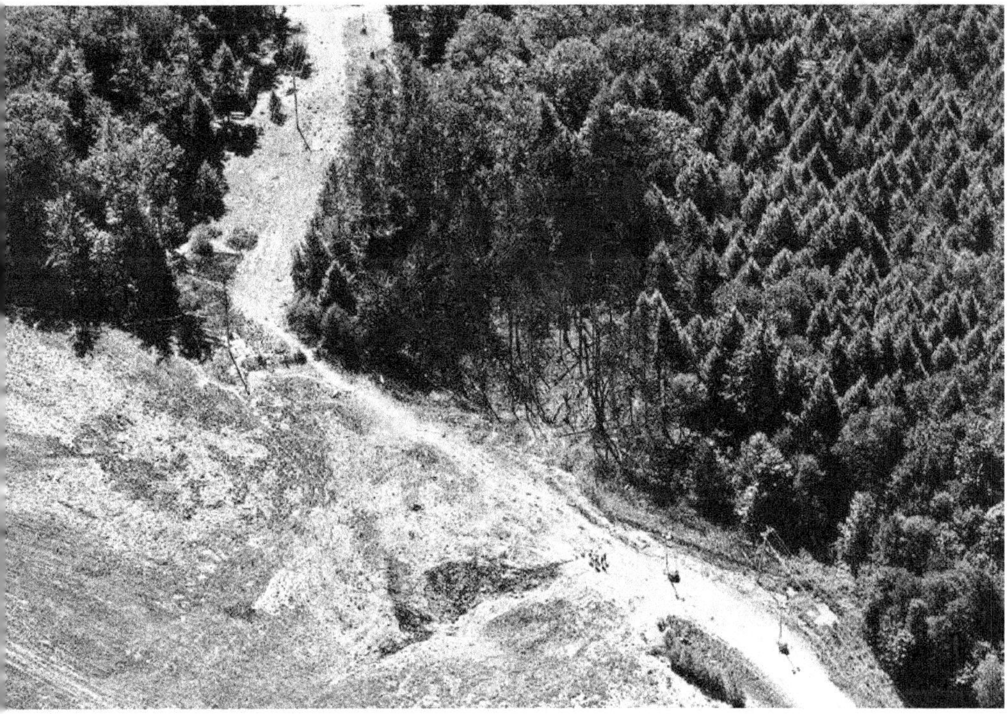

Top left: Repairing the Pentagon
Lower left: Comm and Center

At CIA Headquarters, Director George Tenet ordered the building evacuated. Senior CIA leaders relocated to a structure nearby. Officers working in the Counterterrorism Center stayed to direct analysis and operations. Directorate of Support officers quickly set up computers and phones in an empty conference room that would soon function as the command center.

Many involved in the Agency's counterterrorism efforts say September 11th was the worst day of their lives. But it reaffirmed their commitment to do everything possible to fight the scourge of al-Qa'ida. CIA was uniquely positioned to respond having worked against terrorism since the early 1980s. On September 11th, it was ready to meet the requirements of the President and senior policymakers. The 9/11 Commission's final report noted that prior to September 11th "no agency had more responsibility—or did more—to attack al-Qa'ida, working day and night, than the CIA." We had the capability, resources, training, knowledge, and determination to strike back.

02 AFGHANISTAN:
A FOREBODING LAND
FOR OUTSIDERS

Afghanistan is a rugged, beautiful country, from the snow-capped Hindu Kush and the green mountain valleys to the stark landscape of the northern and southern plains. It is home to a tapestry of peoples and cultures, whose histories are those of the ancient powers of the East, from the Median, Persian, Gupta, and Mongol empires. Trade routes from across the ancient world traversed its passes, giving rise to trading centers such as Herat, Kandahar, and Kabul.

Historically, though Middle Eastern and Eurasian languages had terms for Afghanistan, its own people had little sense of nationhood. Political identity tended to rest at much lower levels, such as the tribe, region, or village. Real power in Afghanistan extended as far as a ruler could reach to tax or enforce his will; boundaries set by empires or dynasties meant relatively little. Rebellion, warfare, and defiance of authority proved more enduring than any sense of national cohesion.

Photo: Afghan fighters

CIA & AFGHANISTAN

After the Soviet Union invaded Afghanistan in December 1979, President Carter directed CIA to assist the Afghan mujahidin. CIA came to see that the indigenous Afghan opposition to the Soviets was less an organized movement than widespread opposition by villages and tribes.

Through Pakistan, CIA provided the mujahidin with money, weapons, medical supplies, and communications equipment. Initially the goal was to drain Soviet resources by keeping their forces bogged down. In 1985, CIA shifted from a plan of attrition to one that would help the rebels win. One of the pivotal moments came in September 1986, when the mujahidin used CIA-provided Stinger missiles to

Photo: Local transport in Afghanistan

shoot down three Soviet Mi-24D helicopter gunships. As part of this escalation of financial and materiel support, President Reagan issued new guidance that put CIA into more direct contact with rebel commanders, beginning an era of CIA interaction with tribal and local leaders that continues through the post-9/11 era.

The Soviet withdrawal in 1989 eliminated the key interest that the United States had shared with the mujahidin. The foreign fighters who had joined the Afghan resistance dispersed to other parts of the world, and the local commanders undertook a violent and difficult struggle for control of the country's resources and government, which culminated in Taliban rule.

AL-QA'IDA & THE TALIBAN

In 1996, Usama bin Ladin and other senior leaders of al-Qa'ida moved from Sudan to Afghanistan and began strengthening ties to the Taliban—the brutal government that gave them safe haven. By then, the CIA was tracking al-Qa'ida as a growing threat to US security. After al-Qa'ida bombed the US embassies in Nairobi and Dar es Salaam in 1998, CIA intensified its operations against the terrorist group, in part by reconnecting with Afghan allies from the war against the Soviets. Now known as the Northern Alliance, these Afghans were resisting Taliban rule.

In late 2000, US policymakers asked CIA what additional resources and authorities it would need to pursue al-Qa'ida in Afghanistan. The Agency recommended stronger support for the Northern Alliance and others opposed to the Taliban governance, as well as assistance to those who might capture al-Qa'ida leaders.

This planning laid the groundwork for CIA's aggressive response to the attacks of September 11th. Its experience with rebel commanders and established relationship with the Northern Alliance proved vital to the Agency's post-9/11 operations. On September 12th, CIA briefed the President on a plan to overthrow the Taliban, including a pledge that Agency officers could be posted with Northern Alliance commanders within two weeks.

Top: rebel view of Afghanistan mountain ranges from a Mi-17 helicopter Lower right: rocky mountains of Afghanistan

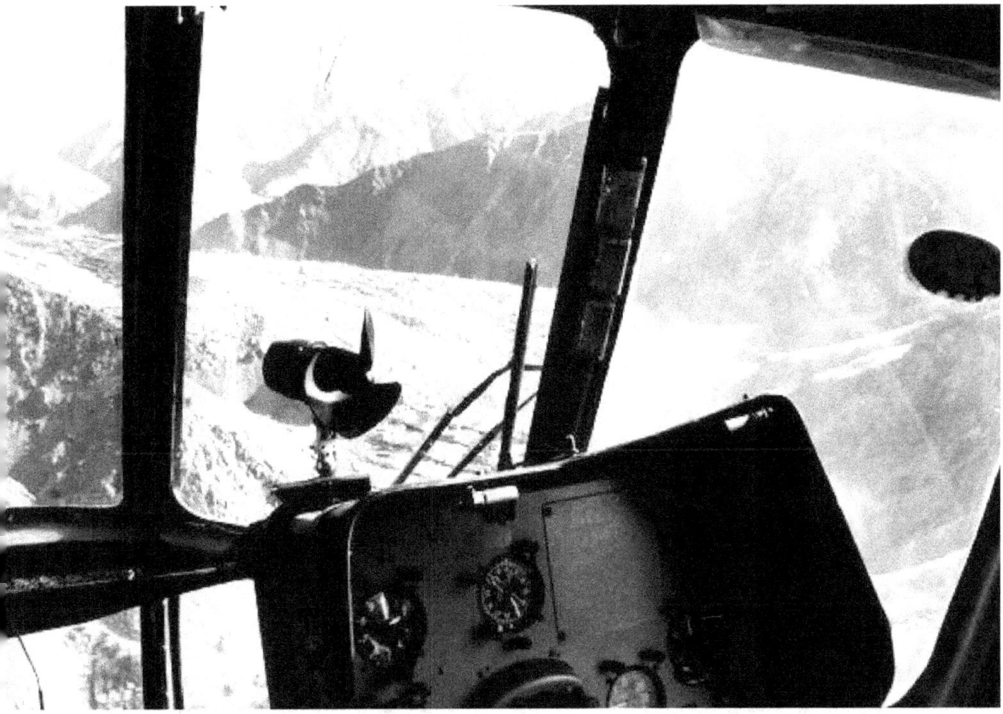

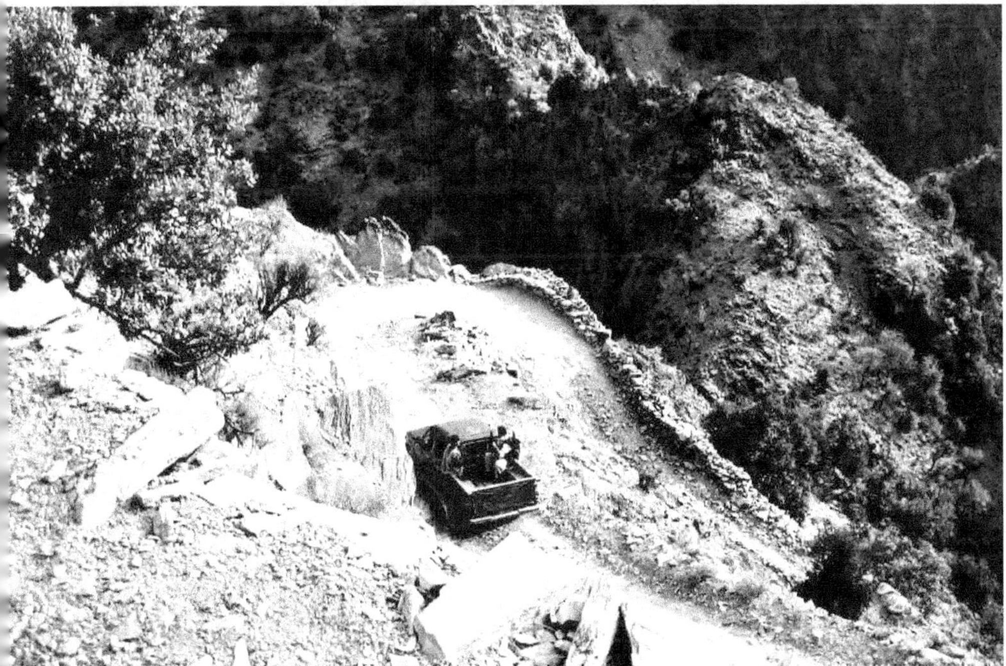

Top photo: Afghanistan landscape.
Right photo: Food supplies from the US Government.

A week after the attack, Director George Tenet told senior Agency managers, "There can be no bureaucratic impediments to success. All the rules have changed...We do not have time to hold meetings to fix problems—fix them—quickly and smartly. Each person must assume an unprecedented degree of personal responsibility."

The first CIA contingent entered Afghanistan on 26 September 2001 and met up with Northern Alliance forces in the Panjshir Valley. In mid-October, another CIA team arrived south of Mazar-e Sharif. By the beginning of November, roughly 100 CIA officers and 300 US Special Forces were in Afghanistan.

03 DCI / GEORGE TENET:
LEADER AND FRIEND

The Director of Central Intelligence (DCI)* served as the head of CIA and the Intelligence Community. In the wake of the September 11th attacks, DCI George Tenet was largely responsible for identifying the terrorists and for planning actions against them. For the latter task, he relied specifically on CIA's ties to Afghan enemies of al-Qa'ida and the Taliban.

A New York native born to Greek immigrant parents, DCI Tenet was a leader whose warmth and concern for others earned him the respect and affection of those he led. His boundless energy allowed him to meet the grueling pace of wartime operations. At posts overseas, he would insist on personally greeting every officer, no matter how long or crowded his own day had been. At Headquarters, Tenet visited officers in the Counterterrorism Center—in part to hear the latest developments, but also to make sure they knew he stood with them and appreciated their sacrifices. One CIA officer described Tenet as "the type of person you always wanted to say 'yes' to." He considered all points of view before making a decision; once it was made, it was final. George Tenet was key to mobilizing and guiding the Agency's comprehensive response to September 11th.

*In 2004, President Bush signed the Intelligence Reform and Terrorism Prevention Act which stretched the Intelligence Community, dividing the position of Director of Central Intelligence and creating a separate position, the Director of National Intelligence, to oversee the Intelligence Community

04 DIRECTORATE OF INTELLIGENCE (DI):
TELL ME WHAT I NEED TO KNOW

Photo: Post-9/11 meeting at Camp David – President George W. Bush, National Security Advisor Condoleezza Rice, Chief of Staff Andrew Card, DCI George Tenet

Tasked with providing information and assistance to policymakers, starting with the President, DI analysts cover issues worldwide, from politics to economics, and personalities to technology and terrorism. CIA's analytic ranks are filled with critical thinkers trained to sift and test information from all sources.

After September 11th, the DI reorganized to focus even more of its efforts on counterterrorism and Afghanistan. Officers who had been covering other parts of the world were reassigned to CTC—the focal point at the Agency for the war on al-Qa'ida. Many of those who went to work on Afghanistan brought valuable experience from other hotspots, such as the Balkans and Iraq. DI analysts hunkered down for the long days and nights ahead. They would work 10 to 12-hour shifts to ensure constant coverage. Some spent the first few days entirely at CIA Headquarters, sleeping on whatever cot or sofa they could find. Walking through the hallways, one could see pizza boxes and makeshift beds everywhere.

Our government's appetite for the latest information was insatiable. For weeks, regional analysts covering Afghanistan provided around-the-clock briefings. DCI Tenet gave the President critical intelligence as events developed. A CTC analyst identified two al-Qa'ida figures on the manifest for Flight 77, confirming that organization's role. Analysts prepared DCI Tenet for marathon planning sessions at Camp David the weekend after the attacks.

New officers arrived to help meet the enormous demands on the Agency. The enthusiasm and vigor of the new analysts was a boost to officers who spent days and nights after September 11th poring over information and putting together the varied pieces.

After a long shift at work, many officers would leave late in the evening or early in the morning. They would drive under overpasses with American flags waving gently in the breeze—reminders of what their long work days were all about.

"No, but we're going to make it right."

–DI officer, asked by his 4-year-old son if he was going to "fix the planes...and the people...and the buildings..."

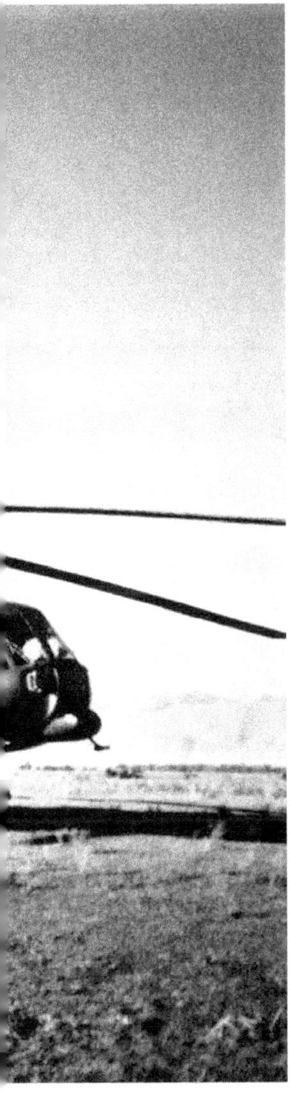

NATIONAL CLANDESTINE SERVICE (NCS): 05

FIRST ON THE GROUND

Immediately after September 11th, at the direction of the President, the National Clandestine Service—then called the Directorate of Operations—took the lead on a secret plan to assemble small teams and deploy them to Afghanistan to partner with the Northern Alliance, overthrow the Taliban, and deny al-Qa'ida its safe haven. At a White House meeting on September 17th, President Bush gave the Agency its orders: "I want CIA to be first on the ground." Paramilitary officers, experts at collecting intelligence in hazardous places, were at the vanguard of CIA's operations.

The seven-man Northern Alliance Liaison Team (NALT) landed on Afghan soil on September 26, 2001, just 15 days after the terrorist attacks. They brought a remarkable range of skills to the mission, including proficiency in Russian, Dari, and Farsi. Building on the Agency's longstanding relationship with the Northern Alliance, the team collected intelligence on the Taliban, reporting the latest developments back to Headquarters every two hours.

Agency officers slept in small, cramped rooms. The team brought 40 pounds of onions and 40 pounds of potatoes with them, but ate mostly local food. Bathroom facilities were rudimentary. Officers slept in long johns to stay warm. One of them broke a toe when a portable electrical generator fell on his foot. He wore flip flops while it healed, even as temperatures began to drop. CIA officers tried hanging their laundry outside, but wet clothes didn't dry well in the Afghan winter. The officers started hanging them up indoors.

Small but highly agile paramilitary mobile teams followed the first NALT, spreading out over the countryside during the day to meet with locals and gather information about the Taliban and al-Qa'ida. In the evenings, they slept outside of town. During that time, one of the teams was approached in a village and asked by a young man to help in retrieving his teenage sister. He explained that a senior Taliban official had taken her as a wife and had sharply restricted the time she could spend with her family. The team gave the man

a small hand-held tracking device to pass along to his sister, with instructions for her to activate it when the Taliban leader returned home. The team responded to her emergency signal, capturing the senior Taliban official and rescuing the sister. The siblings' tearful reunion left the team at a loss for words—a rarity for the normally loud warriors of CIA's Special Activities Division.

06 DIRECTORATE OF SCIENCE AND TECHNOLOGY (DS&T)
UNSURPASSED INGENUITY

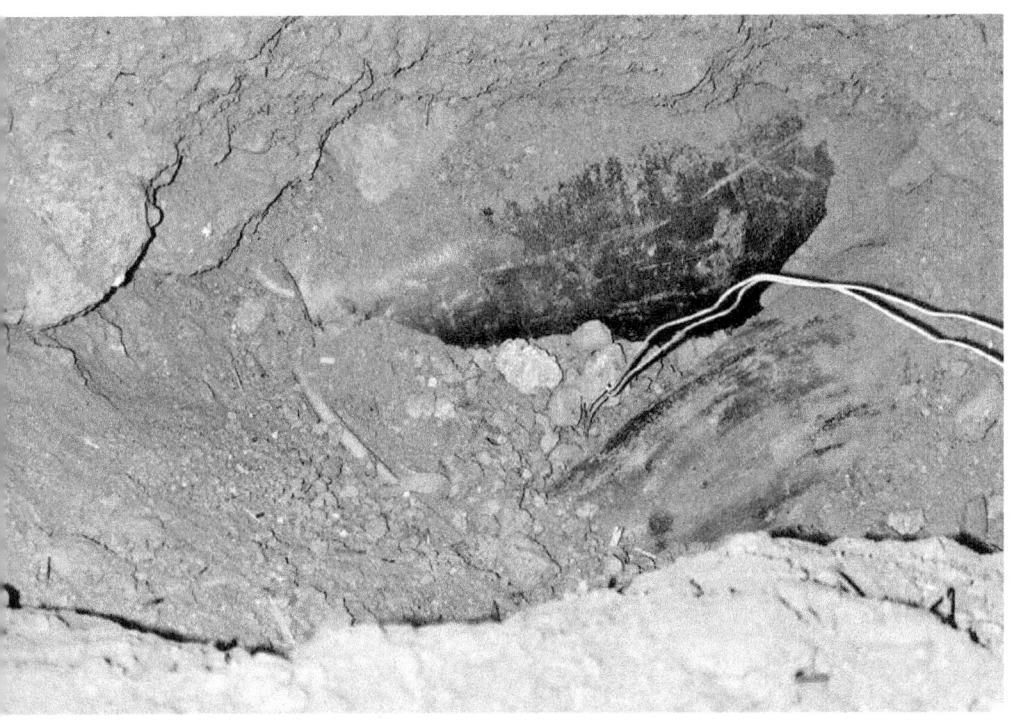
Photo: Mine probing tool and explosives

Scientists, engineers, model makers, and artists are just some of the specialists who serve in the Directorate of Science and Technology. The DS&T deployed its technical expertise after the September 11th attacks to support CIA officers in the field.

IN THE NICK OF TIME…

In late 2001, the DS&T sent a six-member ordnance team to the Afghan city of Kandahar to help dismantle explosive devices which the first CIA teams on the ground were starting to encounter and which were endangering and restricting their operations. They arrived in Kandahar after three grueling days of military transport via C-17 and helicopter and dropped to the floor of the Kandahar base to finally sleep as soon as they arrived. After just two hours of rest, they awakened to the news that an Afghan local was

Photo: Members of CIA Explosive Ordnance Team using mine-probing tools find dozens of mines, artillery shells, and other explosive devices.

in the courtyard saying he had heard that a bomb was hidden in the base compound, in the Palace building right next door, and that it was set to detonate at sunset to mark the end of Ramadan.

That evening, the governor was hosting a celebration to mark the end of Ramadan with allies from all over Afghanistan and US military partners as guests. The DS&T team rushed to sweep the compound, combining years of training and experience with highly technical equipment specially suited to the task. The inspection began on the roof and within minutes the team soon uncovered a 2,500 pound Improvised Explosive Device (IED) discreetly lodged inside the Palace's dirt roof. With the sun setting in the background, the team rendered the IED safe with just minutes to spare and the governor's festivities beginning only feet below.

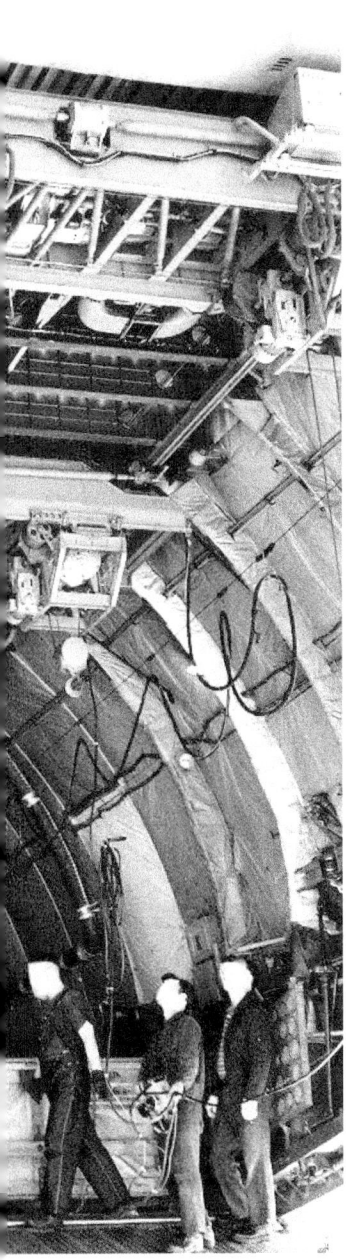

DIRECTORATE OF SUPPORT (DS):
FROM HEADQUARTERS TO THE FIELD,
WHERE THE UNIT NEEDS

 07

The Directorate of Support is prepared to facilitate CIA operations wherever, whenever. Their role is to ensure that officers are safe, secure, healthy, and fully able to carry out CIA's mission worldwide. They support the Agency's workforce at Headquarters, and played a critical role in our response to September 11th. The DS procured equipment at home and delivered it wherever it was needed overseas.

The demands of the mission were constant; one of the logistics officers said she had to accept that her work would never really end. Another officer compared it to high-stress work in retail management during the holiday season—except this job carried considerable personal risk and was all about national security implications, not commissions or a corporate bottom line.

WE NEED CONNECTIVITY...

A communications specialist deployed with the first team into Afghanistan. The officer, and those who followed, worked almost 24 hours a day, 7 days a week. They were the "connectors"—uniting the field with Headquarters to ensure the critical flow of information. The communications officers lived on top of their equipment and caught sleep whenever they could. The job had other challenges, as well—including power outages, the large time difference with Headquarters, and dealing with dirty fuel for generators.

WE NEED A WAREHOUSE...

Teams abroad needed a facility to store equipment, and the Directorate of Support was assigned to build one. DS officers were given one week—just after Thanksgiving—to procure and ship everything needed to build two warehouses. They acquired, packed, and palletized the equipment and loaded it onto a C-17 transport plane. Their gear included 50 by 75 foot structures, power generators, forklifts, and scissor lifts.

The route to Afghanistan was rarely direct. The team had to stop at airports and stay with their equipment on the plane. Sometimes they had to spend a night at an airfield and would play cards to pass the time. The setting was often the belly of their plane, atop a crate lit only by flashlight.

When they landed, the team had three days to build the first warehouse. For security reasons, they worked only during daylight. They got the job done on schedule and finished construction of a second warehouse, completing both jobs a week after the officers had arrived.

Photo: Loading supplies
Previous page: Loading equipment into C-17 transport plane for shipment

WE NEED POWER...

Few operations can get off the ground without electricity, which runs everything from the communications equipment to the coffee maker. To deal with the growing demand for power as more officers deployed to Afghanistan, a DS officer used ingenuity and creativity to locate an existing out-of-use generator in an abandoned building. The officer was thrilled to be able to get it up and running. After several tries, the old machine sputtered to life—an invaluable jolt to the mission.

SEPTEMBER'S
LEGACY **08**

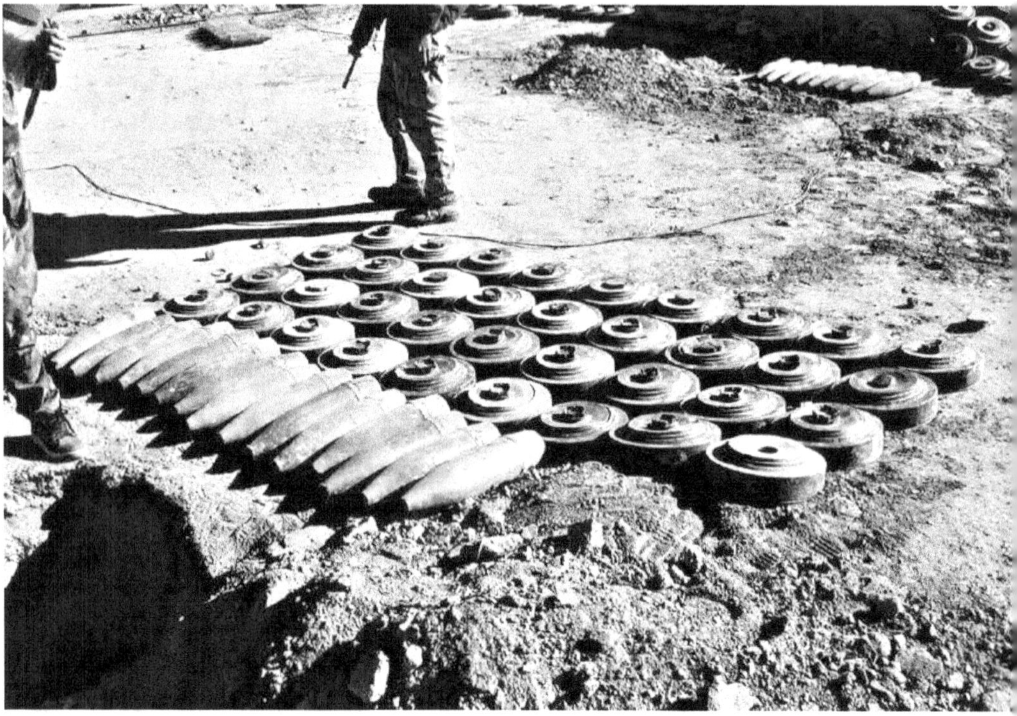

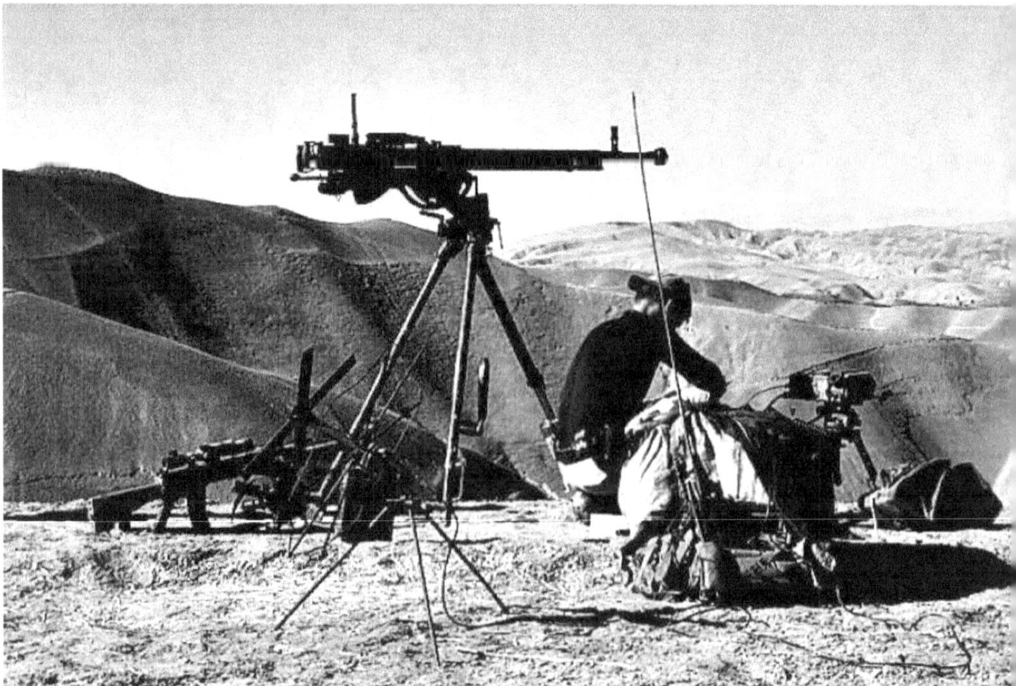

The efforts of CIA officers in the days after September 11th accomplished what this Agency set out to do—overthrow the Taliban, deny al-Qa'ida its safe haven, and provide critical intelligence to policymakers.

CIA officers, like all Americans, are forever shaped by what they experienced on September 11th and in the months that followed. Some of the men and women who shared their stories here have become leaders at this Agency; some continue to work on counter-terrorism; and all serve with heartfelt devotion to the same cause: that such a tragedy never happens again.

The communications officer who was with the first team into Afghanistan brought his family to an Agency ceremony honoring his work. Afterward, his daughter—a college student—told him she wanted to be part of CIA's mission. She now works in the Directorate of Science and Technology.

"Once I got on the plane to come back home, I knew I did everything I possibly could do for this country and our organization... and, in my own head, that is an achievement."

– CIA Communications Officer

Previous page: Mi-17 helicopter used by NALT
Top left: Unearthed mines, artillery shells, and other explosive devices
Lower left: Setting up AN/PEQ-1A SOF laser marker used to identify enemy targets and direct precise delivery of laser-guided ordnance

More than half the workforce has joined the Agency since 2001. The new officers have brought tremendous skill, energy, and dedication to an organization transformed by the terrible events of that fateful day in September. CIA today is a far more collaborative intelligence service - internally, among our Directorates, and externally, with our Intelligence Community colleagues and our foreign liaison partners.

Our people are far more likely to serve abroad, often in dangerous places: one of every seven officers has served at least 90 days in a war zone. That expeditionary approach extends to our analysis, too. More than ever before, our analytic culture encourages exploring alternate scenarios, gaining ground truth from overseas postings, and vigorously challenging long-held assumptions.

Terrorism remains a very real threat to our nation—and our Agency's highest priority. Whether we served at CIA on September 11th or came here because of it, our memories of that day steel us for the hard but deeply satisfying work of keeping our country safe. That, more than anything, is September's legacy.

These are only a fraction of the stories we are able to share with the public. Many others must remain secret.

A PUBLICATION OF THE CENTRAL INTELLIGENCE AGENCY

OFFICE OF PUBLIC AFFAIRS
WWW.CIA.GOV

DECEMBER 2010

www.ingramcontent.com/pod-product-compliance
Lightning Source LLC
Chambersburg PA
CBHW060007300526
45794CB00003B/1130